Dear Parents,

Thank you for having us as part
of your child's development.

What's inside...

- **2** Colours
- Shapes **10**
- Alphabet **20**
- Numbers **50**

Plus!

Certificates, Patterns, Colouring in, Tracing Letters and Numbers.

Let's explore the wonders of the colour wheel!

COLOUR WHEEL

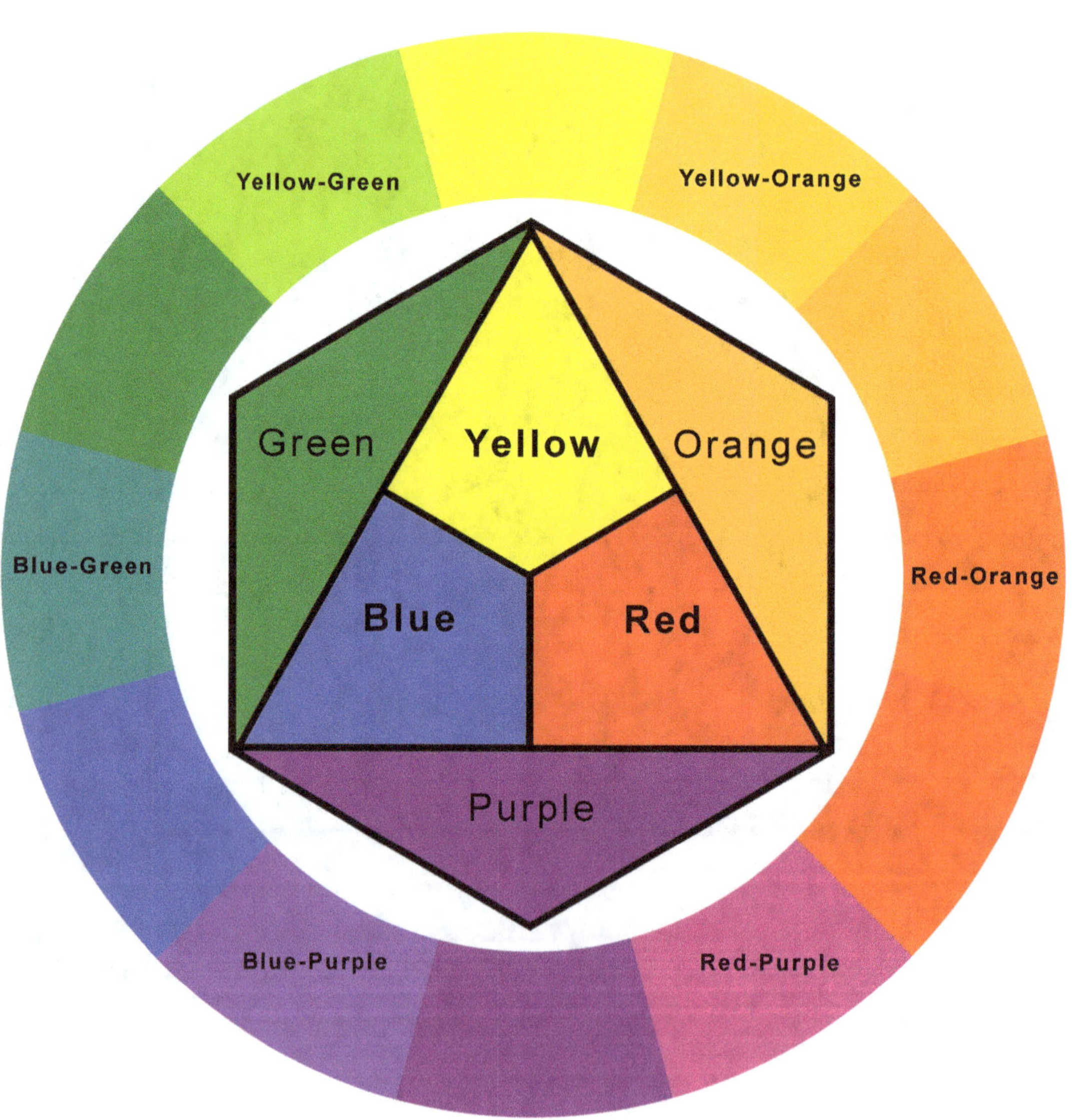

Primary
Colours
Secondary
Colour
Secondary
Colour
Secondary
Colour
Tertiary Colours

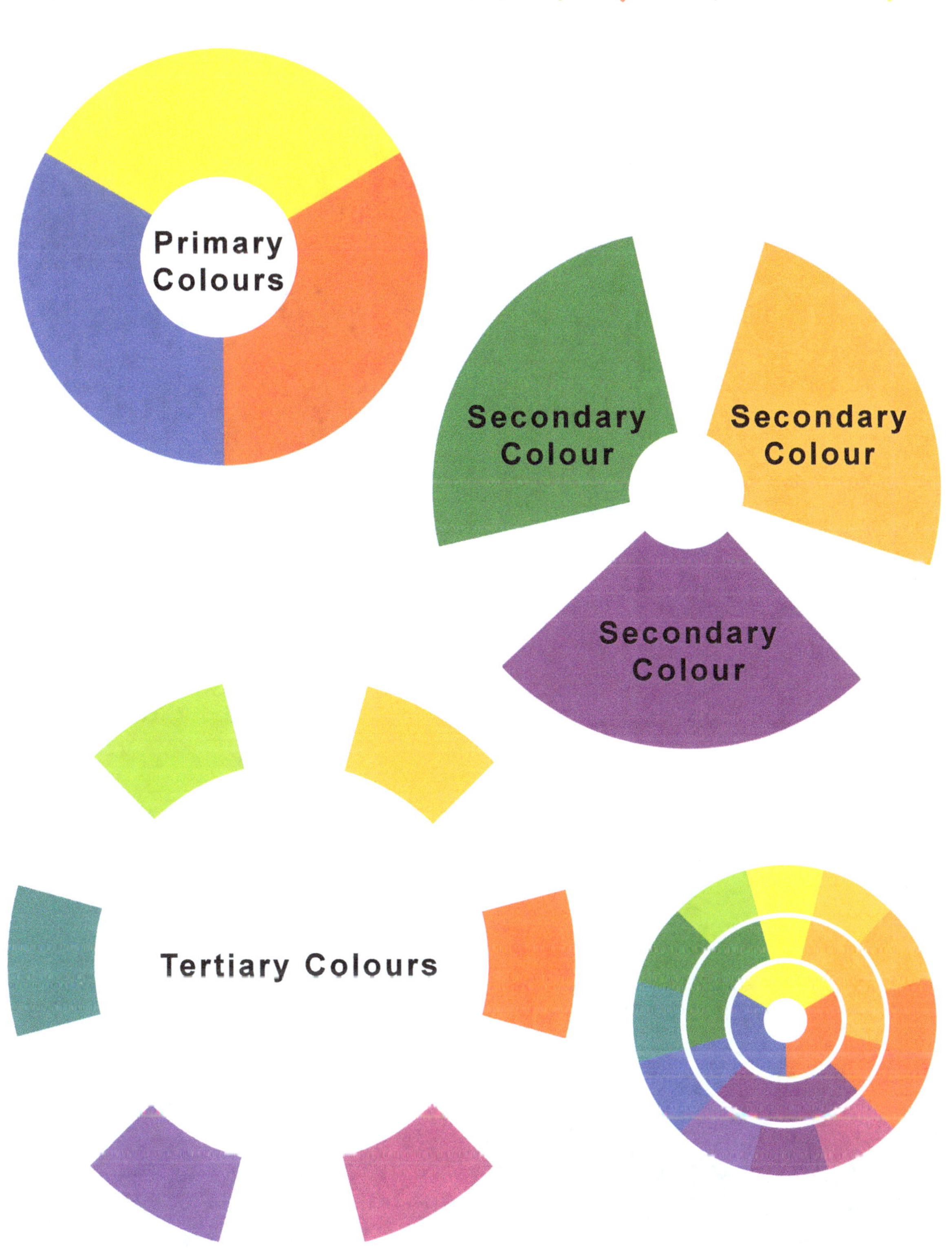

3

THE COLOURS OF THE RAINBOW

1. RED
2. ORANGE
3. YELLOW
4. GREEN
5. BLUE
6. INDIGO
7. VIOLET

FINISH THE RAINBOW

FINISH THE PATTERNS

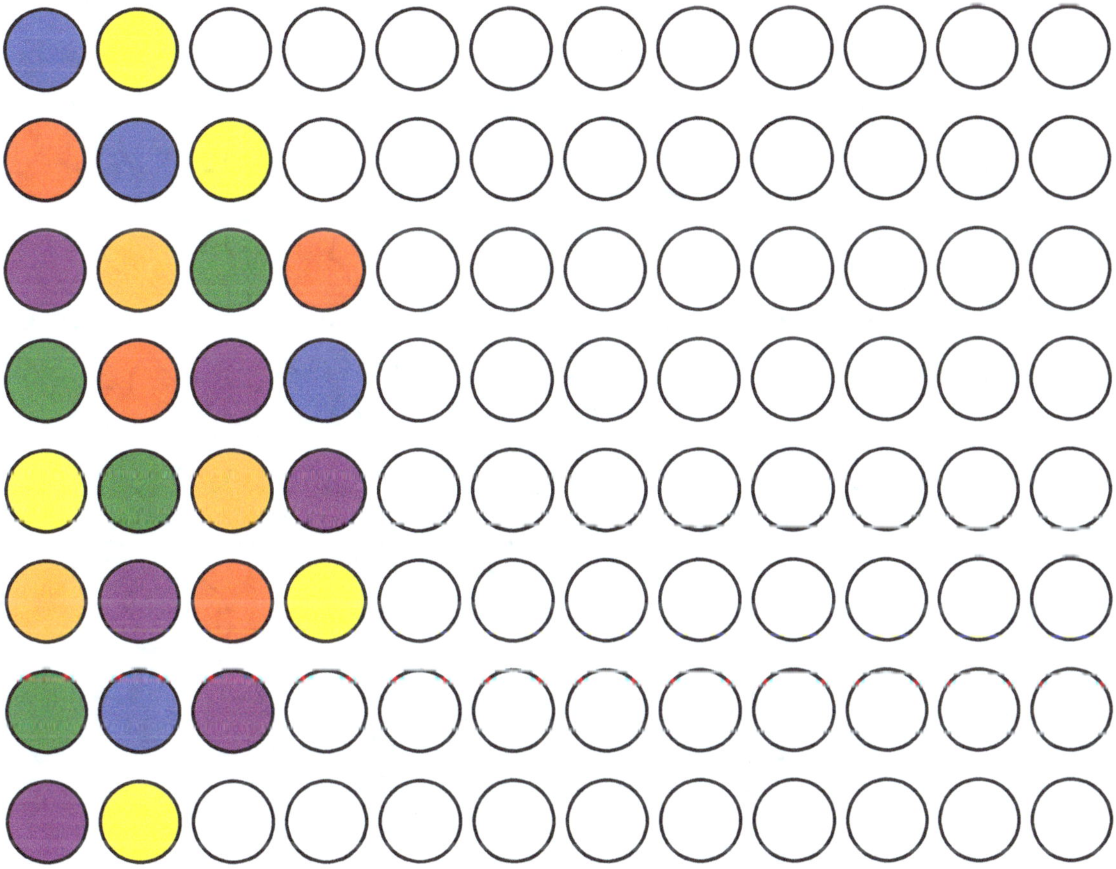

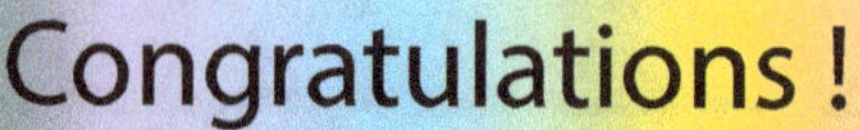

Certificate of Colour Knowledge

This certifies that ___________________ ,
has successfully learnt the primary, secondary,
and tertiary colours through their journey
with Simon and Christopher.

Date: ___________

Explore the magical world of 2D and 3D shapes, tracing their beauty and discovering their secrets!

2D Shapes

Circle
1 Side
Oval
1 Side
Semi Circle
2 Sides
Triangle
3 Sides
Square
4 Sides
Rhombus
4 Sides
Rectangle
4 Sides
Parallelogram
4 Sides

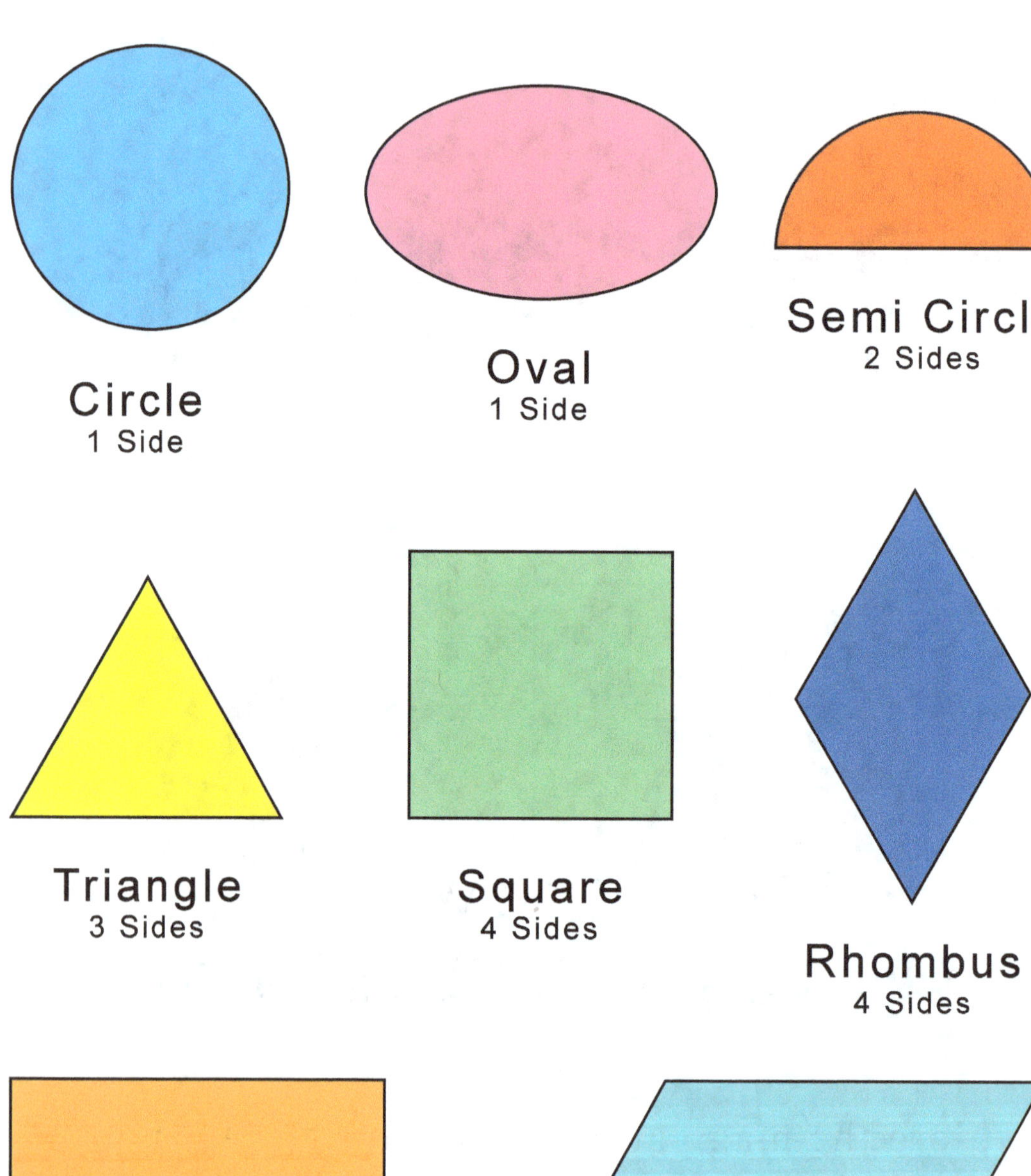

2D Shapes

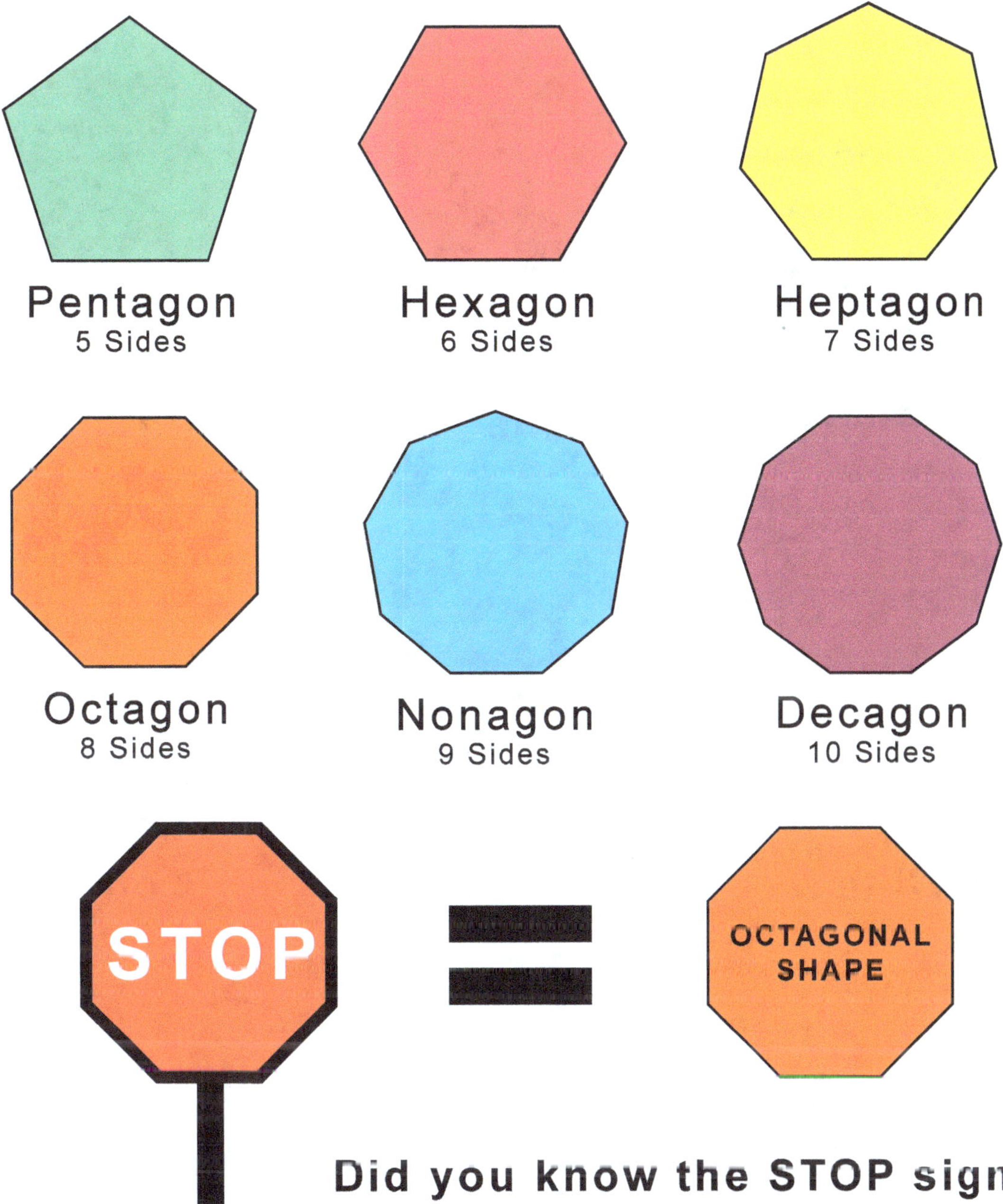

Did you know the STOP sign is an octagonal shape?

3D Shapes

Sphere
Cube
Cuboid
Cylinder
Pyramid
Cone
Triangular Prism
Hexagonal Prism

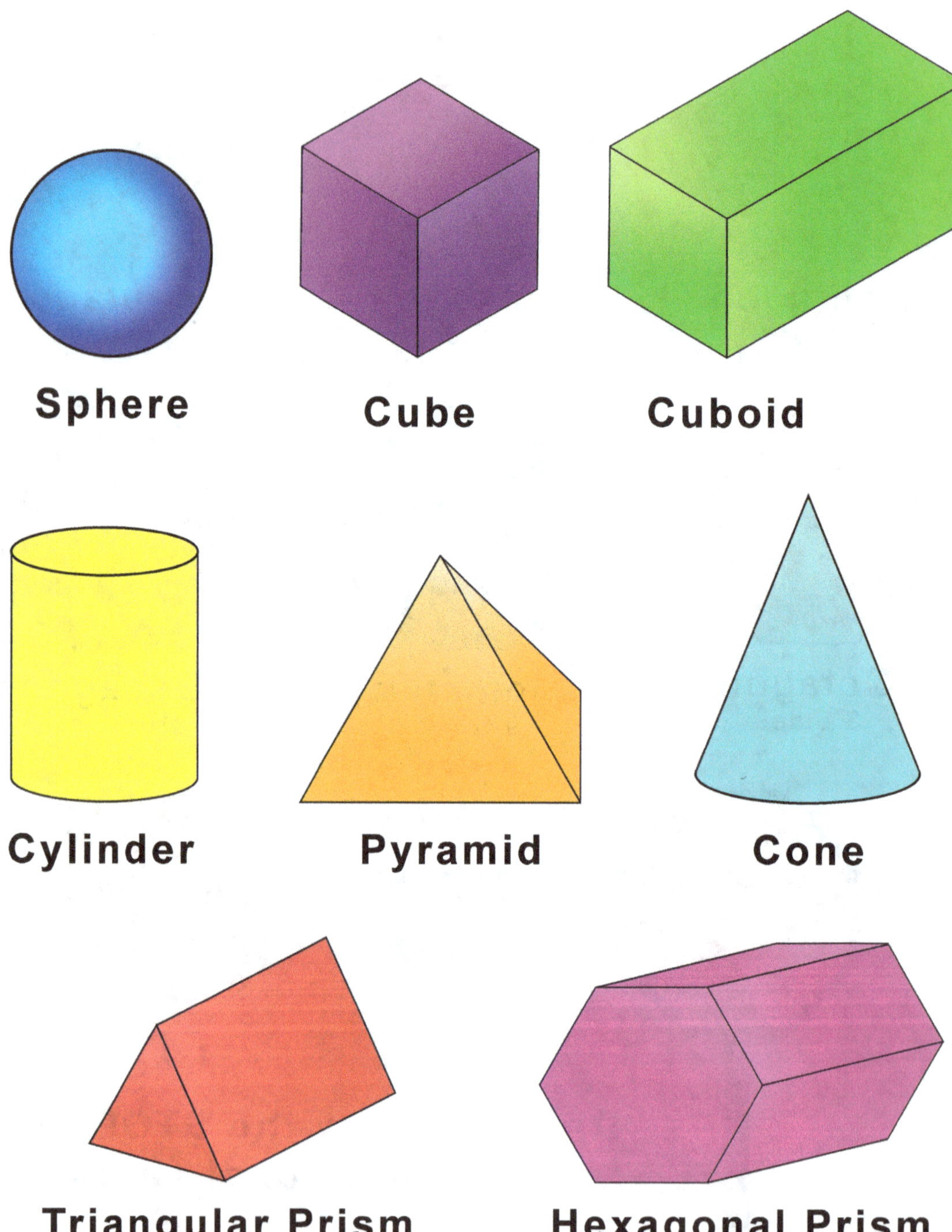

SHAPE TRACING

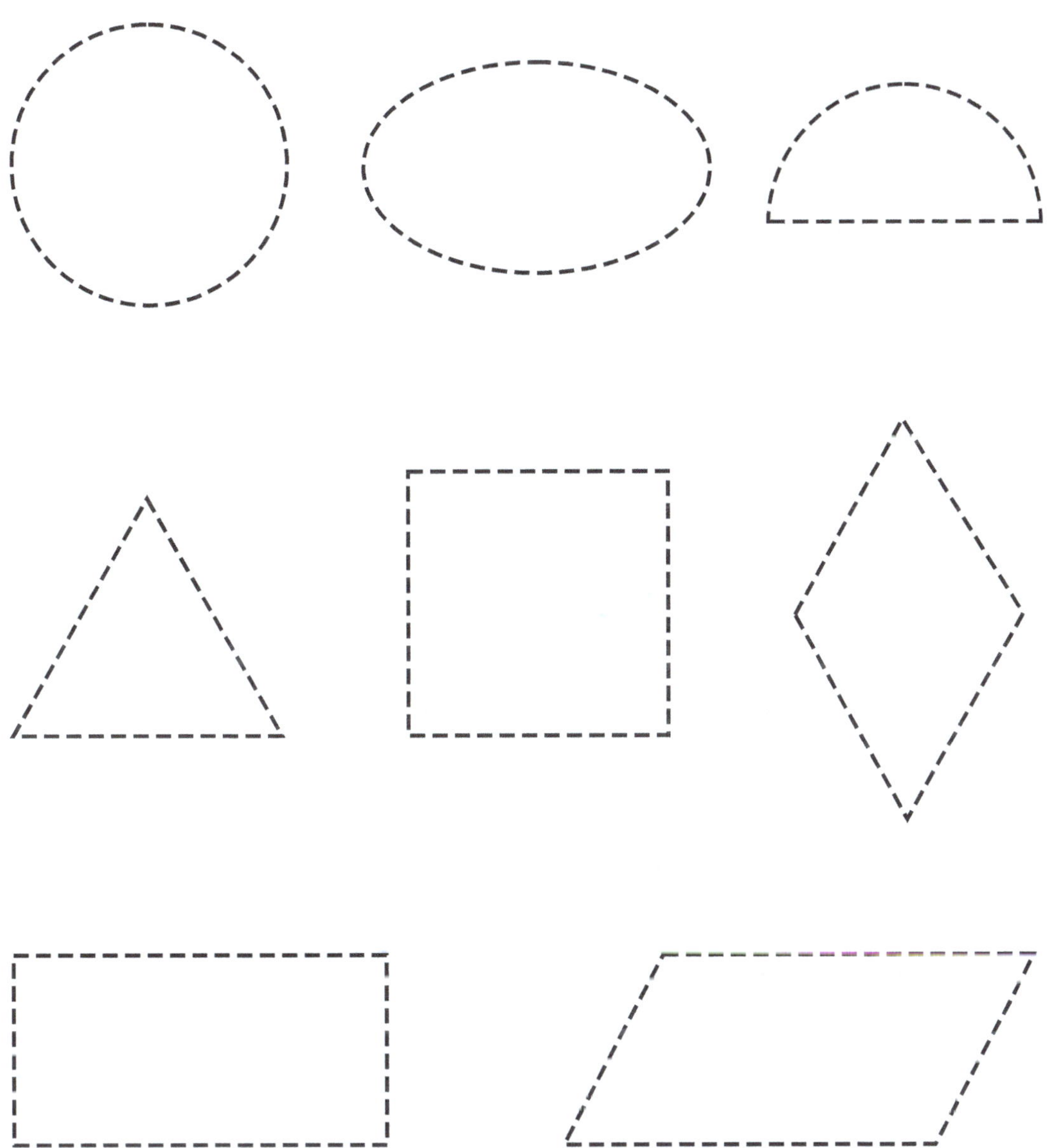

SHAPE TRACING

SHAPE TRACING

TRACE AND COLOUR

TRACE AND COLOUR

Shape Mastery Certificate

This certifies that ________________________ ,
has successfully mastered the fundamentals of 2D
and 3D shapes. With dedication and enthusiasm,
mastery of geometric concepts, including squares,
circles, triangles, cubes, spheres, and more,
has been demonstrated.

Date: ___________

Let's explore all sorts of yummy fruits
from A to Z together!

ALPHABET

A a B b C c

D d E e F f G g

H h I i J j K k

L l M m N n O o

P p Q q R r S s

T t U u V v W w

X x Y y Z z

A a

Apple

a a a a a a a a

a a a a a a a a

A A A A A A A A

A A A A A A A A

Colour in:

Bb

Banana

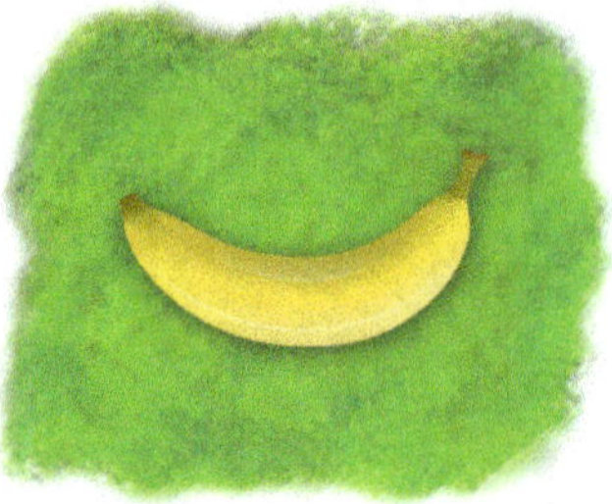

b b b b b b b

b b b b b b b

B B B B B B B

B B B B B B B

Colour in:

BANANA

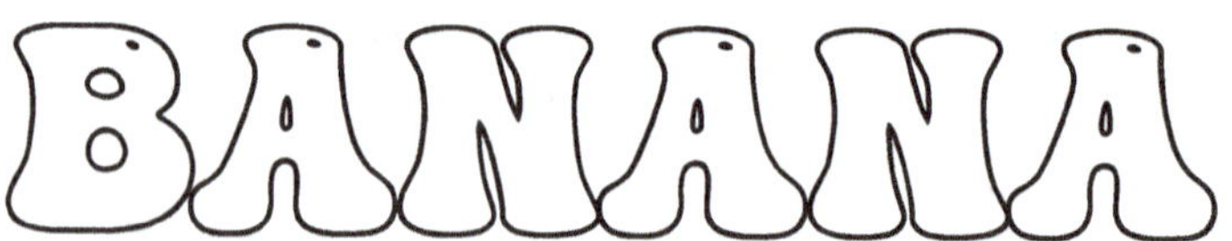

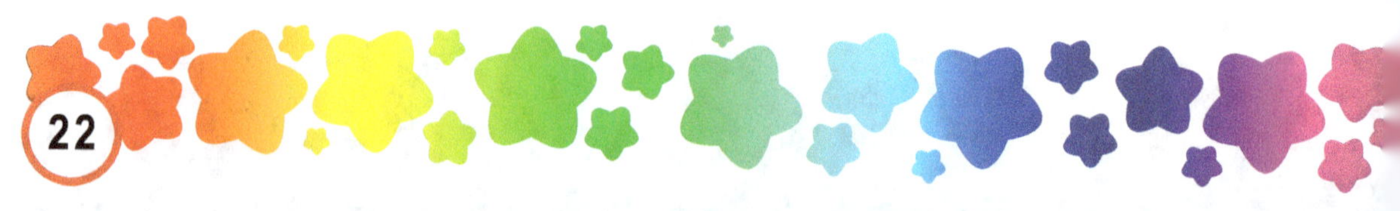

Colour in:

CHERRY

Dd

Dragon fruit

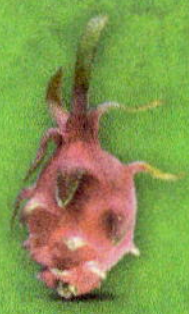

d d d d d d d

d d d d d d d

D D D D D D

D D D D D D

Colour in:

DRAGON FRUIT

Ee

Eggfruit

e e e e e e e e e

e e e e e e e e e

E E E E E E E E E

E E E E E E E E E

Colour in:

EGGFRUIT

Ff

Fig

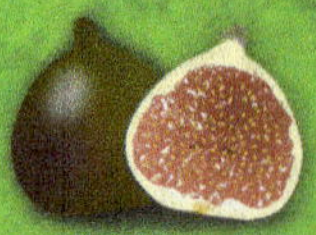

f f f f f f f f f

f f f f f f f f f

F F F F F F F

F F F F F F F

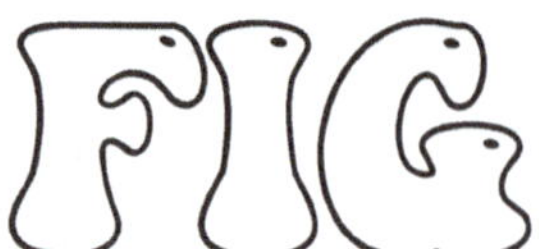

Colour in:

FIG

G g

Grapes

g g g g g g g

g g g g g g g

G G G G G G G

G G G G G G G

Colour in:

GRAPES

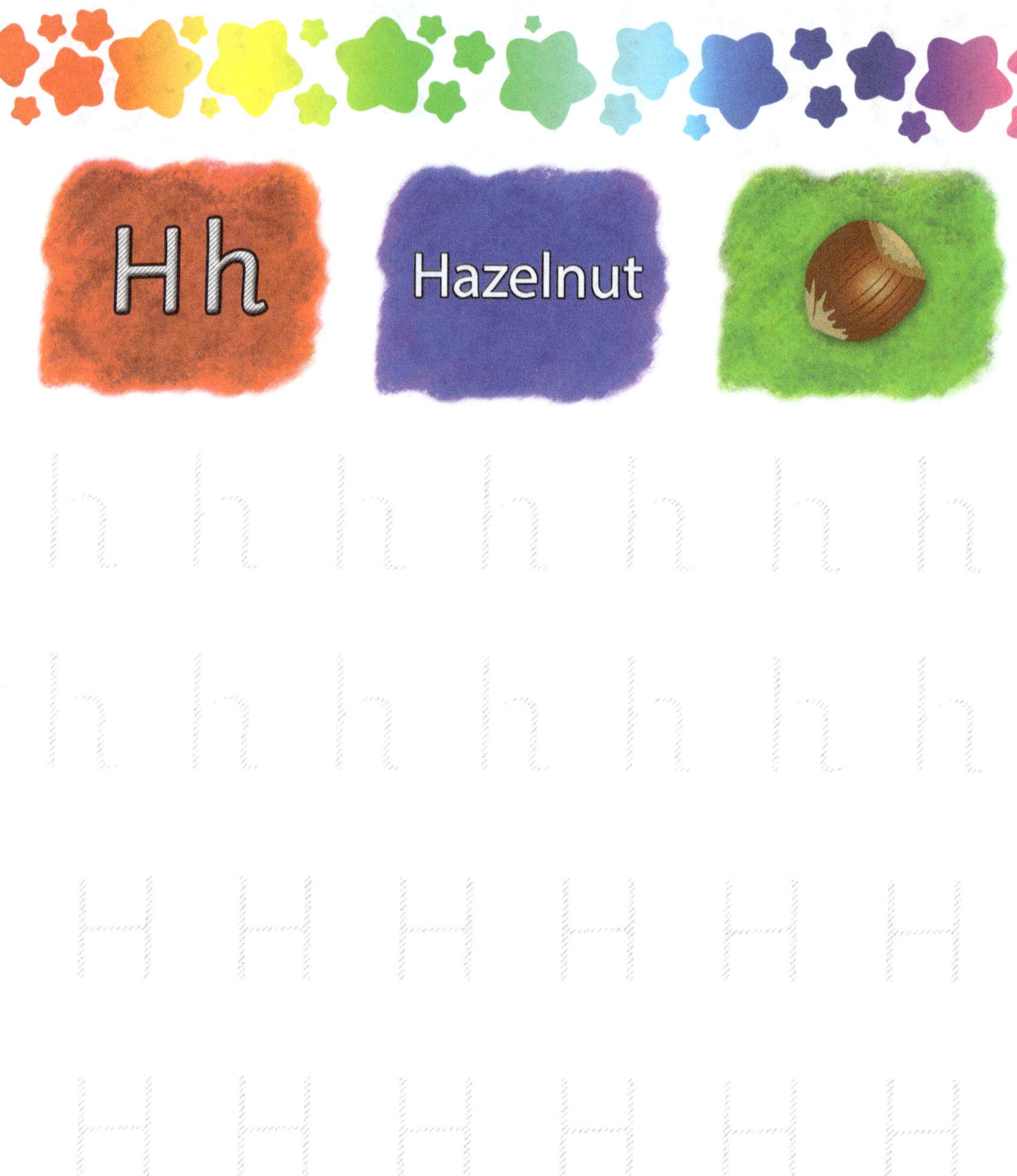

Colour in:

I i

Icaco fruit

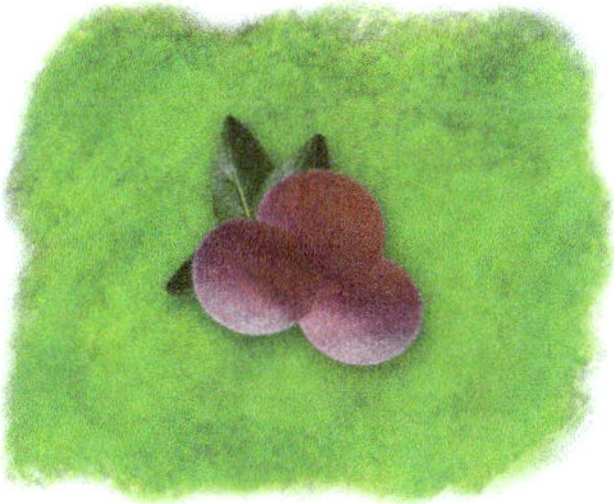

Colour in:

ICACO FRUIT

Colour in:

Kk

Kiwifruit

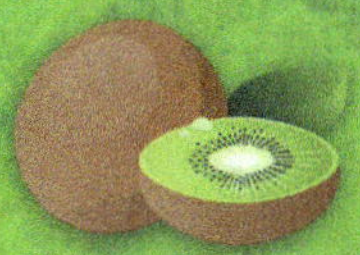

k k k k k k k

k k k k k k k

K K K K K K K

K K K K K K K

Colour in:

KIWIFRUIT

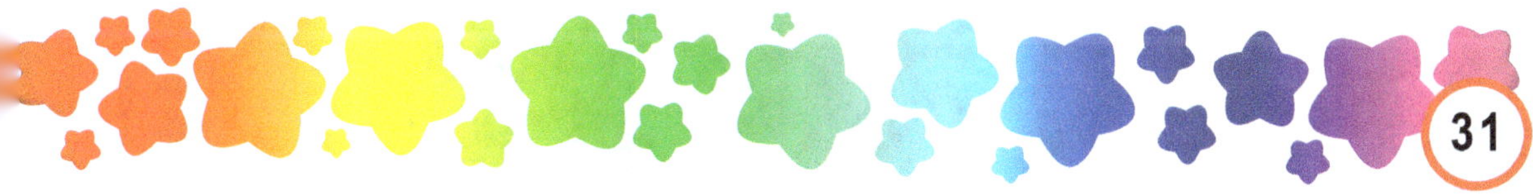

Ll

Lemon

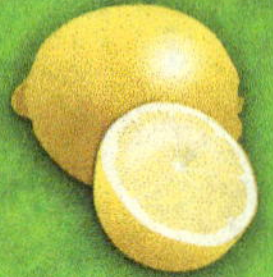

l l l l l l l l l

l l l l l l l l l

L L L L L L L

L L L L L L L

Colour in:

LEMON

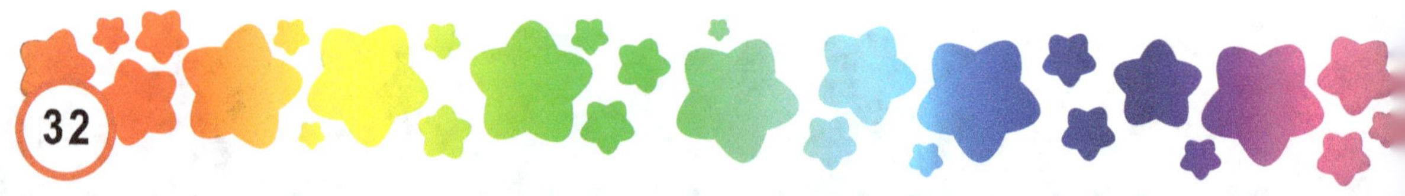

M m

Mango

m m m m m m

m m m m m m

M M M M M M

M M M M M M

Colour in:

MANGO

Colour in:

NECTARINE

Oo

Orange

Colour in:

ORANGE

Pp

Pineapple

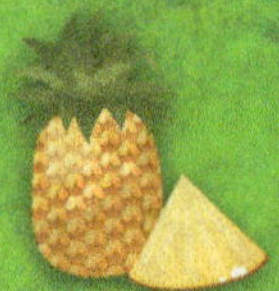

p p p p p p p

p p p p p p p

P P P P P P P

P P P P P P P

Colour in:

PINEAPPLE

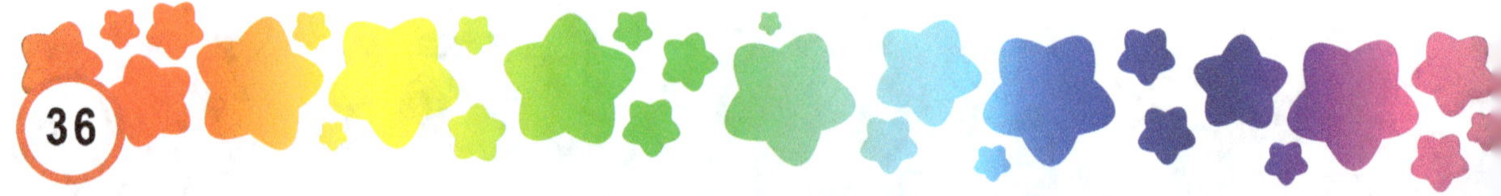

Qq

Quince

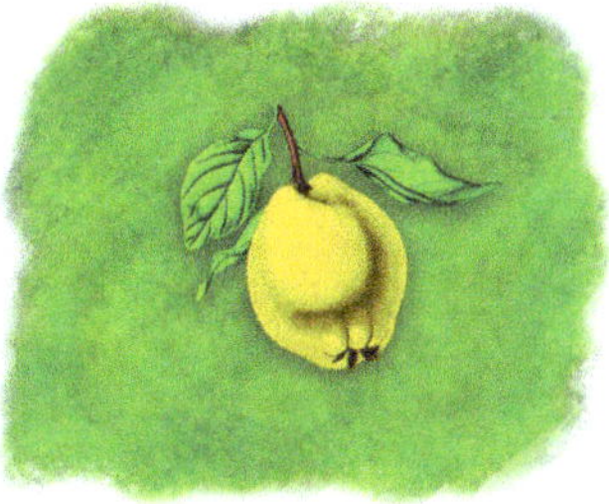

q q q q q q q

q q q q q q q

Q Q Q Q Q Q

Q Q Q Q Q Q

Colour in:

QUINCE

Rr

Raspberry

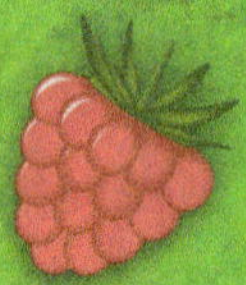

r r r r r r r r

r r r r r r r r

R R R R R R R

R R R R R R R

Colour in:

RASPBERRY

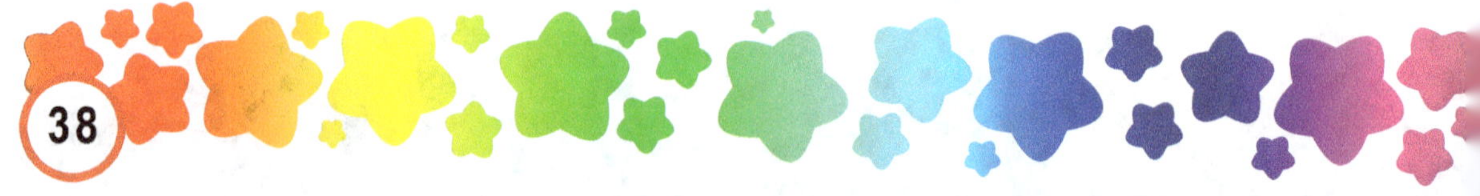

Ss

Strawberry

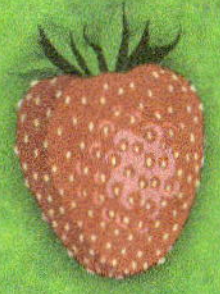

s s s s s s s s

s s s s s s s s

S S S S S S S

S S S S S S S

Colour in:

STRAWBERRY

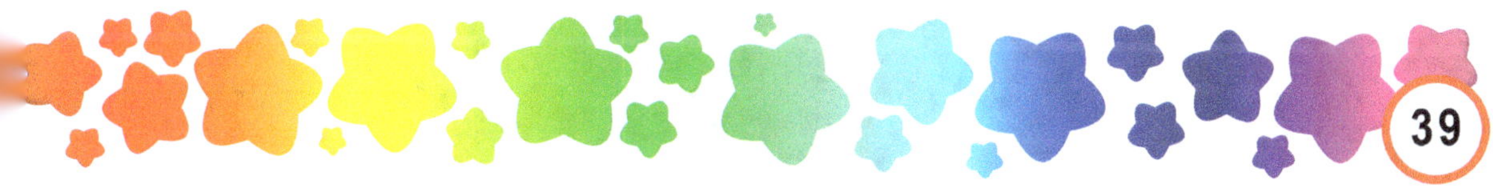

Tt

Tomato

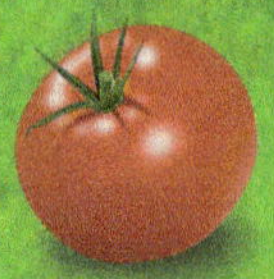

t t t t t t t t

t t t t t t t t

T T T T T T T

T T T T T T T

Colour in:

TOMATO

U u

Ugli

U u u u u u u u u u u

U U U U U U U U U U

U U U U U U U U

Colour in:

UGLI

V v

Vanilla bean

Colour in:

VANILLA BEAN

Ww

Watermelon

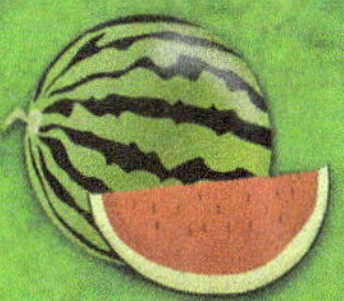

w w w w w

w w w w w

W W W W W

W W W W W

Colour in:

WATERMELON

Colour in:

Yy

Yucca fruit

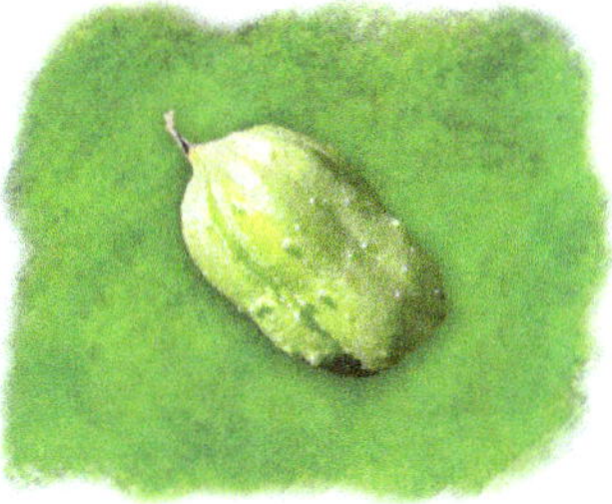

y y y y y y y

y y y y y y y

Y Y Y Y Y Y Y

Y Y Y Y Y Y Y

Colour in:

YUCCA FRUIT

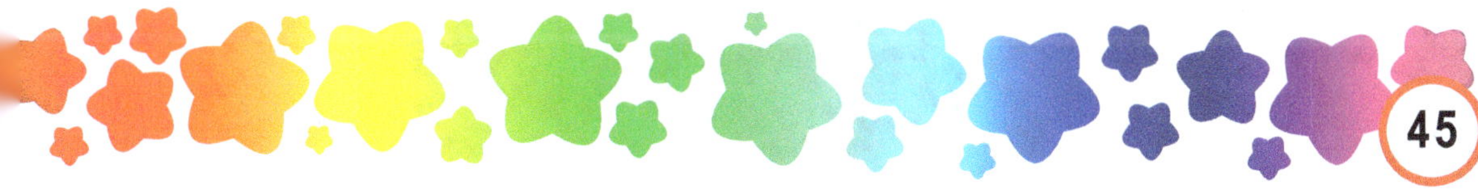

Zz

Zucchini fruit

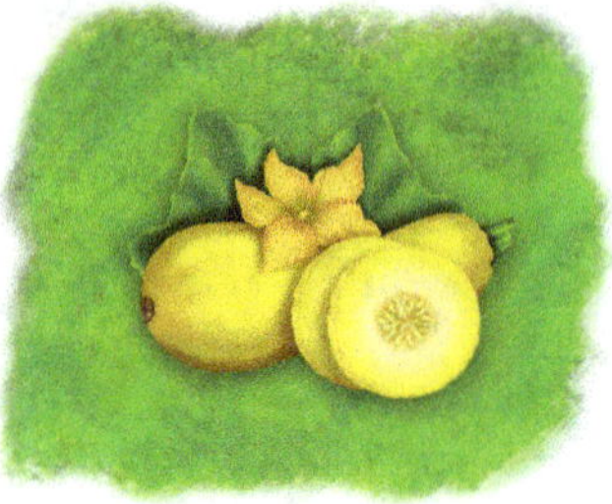

z z z z z z z z

z z z z z z z z

Z Z Z Z Z Z Z

Z Z Z Z Z Z Z

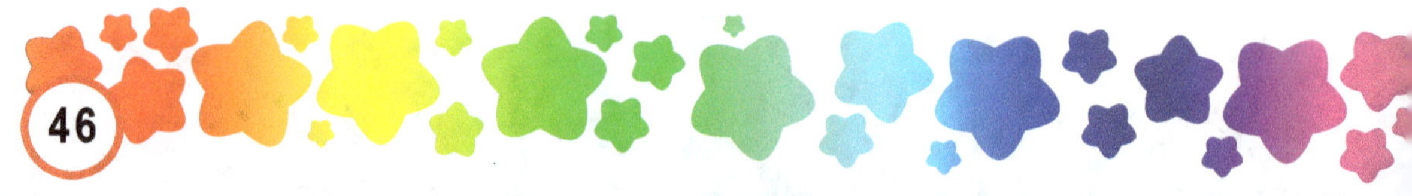

Colour in:

ZUCCHINI FRUIT

Aa Bb Cc
Dd Ee Ff Gg
Hh Ii Jj Kk
Ll Mm Nn Oo
Pp Qq Rr Ss
Tt Uu Vv Ww
Xx Yy Zz

Alphabet Mastery Certificate

This certifies that ___________________________ ,
has successfully learned the alphabet with fruits
corresponding to each letter from A to Z and is
hereby awarded this certificate in recognition of
their dedication and achievement.

Date: __________

Jump into the exciting universe of numbers
from 0 to 10, counting and tracing them together!

Numbers

0
Zero
No Apples

1

One

Apple

2

Two

Apples

3 Three Apples

4

Four

Apples

4 4 4 4 4 4 4

4 4 4 4 4 4 4

4 4 4 4 4 4 4

4 4 4 4 4 4 4

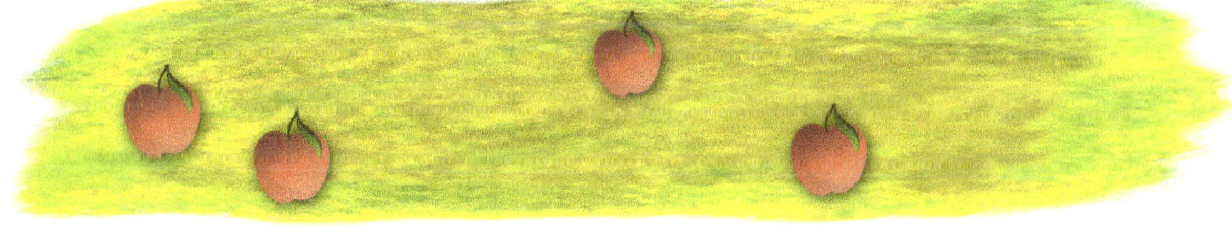

5

Five

Apples

6   Six   Apples

7 Seven 

8

Eight

Apples

9

Nine

Apples

10 Ten Apples

9 8 3 5
6
10 2 1 4 0 7

Certificate of Number Mastery

This certifies that _____________________,
has successfully learned the numbers from
0 to 10 and is hereby awarded this certificate
in recognition of their dedication and
achievement.

Date: ________